the Boys' Summer book

Buster Books

Written by Guy Campbell
Illustrated by Paul Moran
Edited by Sally Pilkington
Designed by Zoe Quayle

Cover illustrated by Nikalas Catlow

First published in Great Britain in 2010 by Buster Books,
an imprint of Michael O'Mara Books Limited,
9 Lion Yard, Tremadoc Road, London SW4 7NQ

A CIP catalogue record for this book is available from the British Library.

ISBN: 978-1-906082-79-6

2 4 6 8 10 9 7 5 3 1

www.mombooks.com/busterbooks

This book was printed in March 2010 at L.E.G.O., Viale dell'Industria 2, 36100, Vicenza, Italy.

CONTENTS

SUMMER SPACE GETAWAY

Take a trip to the puzzle planet for a summer that is out of this world.
All the answers are on page 62.

SPOT THE FLUGROVIAN

Can you spot the Flugrovian among this bunch of alien critters? Flugrovians have five eyes, but no tail. They have some hair on their heads, but no wings. They are also very, very smelly – but luckily you can't tell that from the picture.

SPACE ZOO

Human beings aren't the only animals to venture into space. Animals have been sent into space for over 60 years. The first to go into space were fruit flies in 1947, followed by a monkey called Albert in 1949. Eight years later a dog called Laika was sent up by the Russians. Since then lots of animals have been sent into orbit including ants, frogs, mice, rats and even fish.

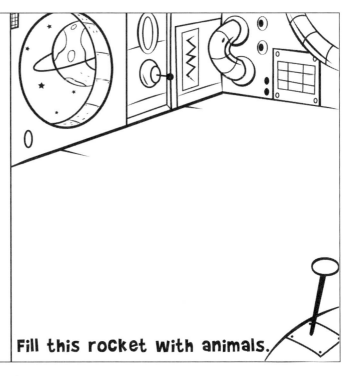

Fill this rocket with animals.

CRYSTAL CAPER

To fix your damaged spacecraft, you need to get a crystal from the cave. You have a crystal-seeking piglet to help you. On your way to the crystal, if your path is blocked by pig-eating cats, you can't pass, but you can pass the crystal-munching dogs.

Cat

When you reach the crystal, leave the pig behind and return to your spacecraft. Now it is safe for you to pass the pig-eating cats, but avoid the crystal-munching dogs.

Dog

Good luck!

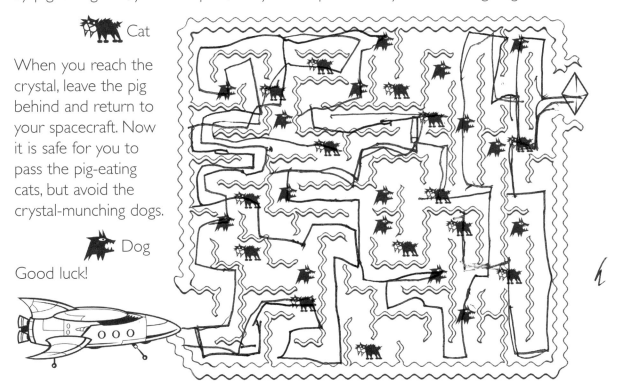

FIX THE MAINFRAME

Can you put the crystal in the right socket, and fix the ship? Choose very carefully.

The crystal must be put in a white socket in a row with two grey sockets and in a column with two black sockets.

MAKE YOUR OWN POWERBOAT

Why not take up powerboat racing this summer? Make your very own high-speed powerboat to race across your bathtub or a paddling pool.

You will need:

- an empty plastic tub • a balloon
- a rubber band • a bendy straw
- scissors • modelling clay

1. Cut the bendy straw in half and keep the bendy end. This will be the exhaust pipe for your boat's 'engine'.

2. Pull the neck of the balloon over the drinking end of the straw, so that it reaches 2 centimetres before the beginning of the bend. Secure it with a rubber band.

3. Place a lump of modelling clay on the outside of your tub towards the bottom-middle of one of the narrower sides.

4. Using the point of your scissors, carefully push through from the inside of your tub into the modelling clay. (Ask an adult to help you with this.) Make the hole just big enough for your straw to fit through.

5. Remove the modelling clay and push the straw through the hole so that the balloon is inside the tub.

6. Press some modelling clay on to the bottom of your boat. This will help to sink the straw below the surface of the water and make it go faster.

7. Squash some more modelling clay on to the outside of your tub, around where your straw pokes through. This will hold the straw in place and make a seal to stop water getting into your boat.

8. Your boat is nearly ready to race. Blow through the straw to inflate the balloon until it fills the tub. Cover the end of your straw with your thumb, to stop the air escaping.

9. To start your powerboat, place it on to the surface of the water and uncover the end of the straw to let the air escape. Watch it speed away.

ANCHORS AWAY!

Can you find which anchor belongs to which boat in this moored maze? Check your answers on page 62.

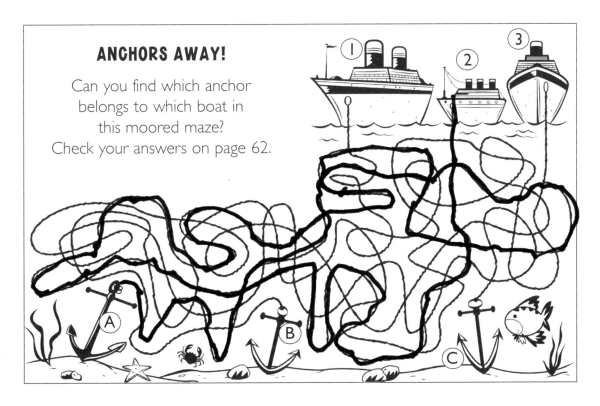

AWESOME ANIMAL QUIZ

Answer the questions below to test you and your friends' knowledge about all things animal. Write each player's answers – A, B, C or D – in the scorecard on the opposite page. All the answers are on page 62.

1. Which furry, hopping animal has a fluffy tail and lucky feet?

   A. Rabbit
   B. Kangaroo
   C. Lemur
   D. Badger

2. Which animal takes part in the sports of showjumping and polo?

   A. Camel
   B. Horse
   C. Dog
   D. Reindeer

3. On which of the following are you most likely to find a polar bear?

   A. Sand
   B. Ice
   C. A bicycle
   D. Television

4. Which country's people take their nickname from the kiwi bird?

   A. Wales
   B. New Zealand
   C. Egypt
   D. France

5. What kind of animal is boy wizard Harry Potter's pet, Hedwig?

   A. Rat
   B. Cat
   C. Toad
   D. Owl

6. Which cat is the fastest land-mammal on the planet?

   A. Lion
   B. Tabby
   C. Cheetah
   D. Tiger

7. Which is the biggest land-based animal in the world?

   A. Field mouse
   B. Donkey
   C. Hippo
   D. Elephant

8. Which black bird is also the name of a piece on a chessboard?

   A. Rook
   B. Emu
   C. Flamingo
   D. Toucan

9. Which sea creature has eight arms?

A. Seahorse
B. Dolphin
C. Octopus
D. Barnacle

11. How many bones are there in a giraffe's neck?

A. 7
B. 17
C. 27
D. 77

10. Which of these creatures is most likely to have a sting in its tail?

A. Crocodile
B. Scorpion
C. Hamster
D. Cobra

12. Which animal has a tongue longer than its body?

A. Python
B. Chameleon
C. Giraffe
D. Blue whale

Question	Player One	Player Two	Player Three	Player Four
1				
2				
3				
4				
5				
6				
7				
8				
9				
10				
11				
12				
TOTAL SCORE				

TAKE THE 'HOUSE OF CARDS' CHALLENGE

Give boredom the red card this summer and become a master builder with this 'house of cards' challenge.

CHALLENGE ONE:
The Trestle

The basic card house is made by leaning two cards against each other so they make a tall triangle. Put two triangles side by side and gently place another card flat on top. This is a trestle – the building block of a house of cards.

Top Tip. Building with cards is much easier on a carpet than on a hard floor.

CHALLENGE TWO:
The Great Pyramid

Put two card trestles side by side and link them together by placing another card to overlap the join where the roofs meet. Build another trestle next to this one, overlapping the roofs as before. To build another floor, build another trestle carefully on top. You will need a steady hand for this.

Keep adding to your pyramid until it falls down or you run out of cards!

CHALLENGE THREE:
Deck Domino Race

Have you ever lined up dominoes and then knocked them all over? It is even more fun with cards! Line up triangles of cards, close enough together so that when you push one over, the next triangle will fall, and the next, and the next. If you have a lot of cards you can make a long, long line of them.

If you and a friend set up lines or 'tracks' the same length, you can race. Prepare your tracks, then push the first triangle over and see whose track tumbles all the way to the end the fastest!

Top Tip. If you are making a very long line, leave a gap every 50 centimetres so that if a card triangle accidentally falls, it won't take out your whole track. When your lines are finished go back and fill in the gaps.

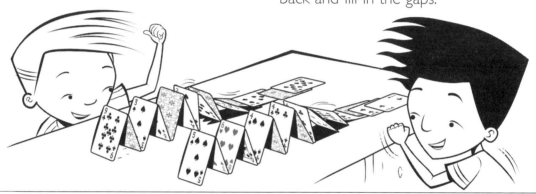

CHALLENGE FOUR:
The Colosseum of Rome

The Colosseum in Rome, Italy is a giant stone building built over a thousand years ago. It took many men many years to construct. You can build your own Colosseum out of cards much faster, but you will need lots of cards. See if you can pick up some old packs in charity shops or car boot sales.

To build your Colosseum, make a circle of trestles 50 centimetres across. To make your circle more stable overlap the roofs of your trestles with more cards. Once you have built this and it is quite stable, add your next floor on top.

If you have lots of cards, make your ground floor circle bigger than 50 centimetres across. If you aren't sure if you have enough cards, start with a smaller circle and add as many floors as you can.

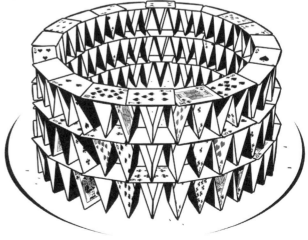

PENS AT THE READY

Whether you are on a long car journey or waiting at the airport, be sure to keep a pen and paper handy for games – time will fly.

BOXING MATCH

You will need two players for this game. To begin, draw a grid of dots on your page measuring seven dots by seven dots like the one shown below.

Take it in turns with your opponent to draw a single line that connects two dots. The line must be either horizontal or vertical – no diagonal lines allowed.

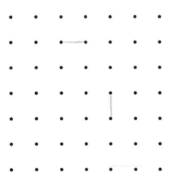

The aim of the game is to complete more boxes than your opponent. When it's your turn, if you find three lines around a box you can finish it with your line and make it yours. Stake your claim by writing the first letter of your name inside. Each time a player completes a box, he can take another turn.

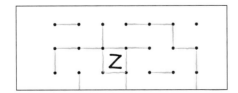

When all the dots have been joined up, count up how many boxes each player has and the person with the most, wins.

Z	Z	Z	Z	Z	S
Z	Z	Z	Z	Z	S
S	S	Z	Z	Z	Z
S	S	Z	Z	Z	S
S	S	Z	Z	S	S
S	S	Z	Z	S	S

Top Tip. Why not play a really long game with a board measuring 20 dots by 20 dots?

BOX CLEVER

Can you find a place to draw your line that doesn't allow your opponent to complete a square?

Check your answer on page 62.

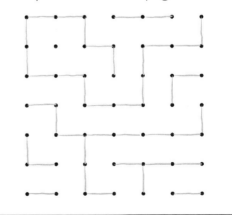

CRAZY SUMMER CONSEQUENCES

You will need two or more players for this game. Each player needs a piece of paper and a pen.

To begin, each player must draw a funny head in the top quarter of his page. The head can be of anything or anyone you like, but don't let anyone see what you are drawing.

When you have finished your drawing, fold down your paper to cover over the head leaving just the two lines of the neck showing. Swap drawings with another player and draw a body and arms on to the neck, in the next quarter of the page. Again, don't let anyone see. Fold your paper over your drawing as you did before and pass your paper on to the next player for them to draw the bottom half of the body and the legs. Pass your picture on again and draw the feet.

When you have drawn the feet of your crazy creation, pass on your paper and then take it in turns to unfold your picture to reveal the funny figure.

A FLICK TO THE FINISH

You will need two players, a piece of paper and two differently coloured felt-tip pens for this game.

Hold the felt-tip pen vertically with one finger on the end, and the tip resting on the paper. Press down with your finger and make the pen flick off, making a line on the paper like this:

This is your start line. Draw a race track that begins and ends at the start line, like the one shown here.

Place your felt-tip pen on the start line and flick it as you did before, following the direction of the race track.

Take it in turns to flick, placing your pen at the end of your previous line.

First player to make it back to the start line, wins!

BECOME A SUMMER SUPER SLEUTH

Get a group of friends together to play these great games where detectives and criminals cross swords to see who's the smartest!

THE TONGUE OF TERROR

You will need at least four players for this game.

Decide on one person to be the Detective and ask him to leave the room. While he is gone decide together who is going to be the Murderer. Ask the Detective to come back in.

The Murderer then has to 'kill' as many people as he can by sticking his tongue out at them without the Detective catching him. Each Victim must immediately die a dramatic death. If the Murderer manages to kill everyone without the Detective catching him, he wins. If the Detective names the killer before everyone is dead, he wins!

THE USUAL SUSPECTS

You will need at least five players for this game, a bag, and a pen and piece of paper for each player.

Ask each player to write down the answers to the following questions: 'What is your favourite food?', 'What is your favourite film?', 'What colour is your hair?', 'What colour are your socks?' and other similar questions. Put all the answer sheets into a bag and then ask one player to be the Detective.

The Detective must choose a piece of paper from the bag and say: 'The Suspect matches the following description'. He then reads each item on the list one at a time. The first person to guess the identity of the Suspect wins, and gets to be the Detective for the next round.

TOUGH QUESTIONS

You will need at least four players for this game, a pen and a piece of paper.

Write the word 'Killer' on a piece of paper. Choose one person to be the Detective and send them out of the room. Now, decide who is going to be the Killer and give that person the piece of paper to hold in his hand. The Detective returns and has to ask three questions to discover who the Killer is. The questions must be directed at one player and can only have 'Yes' or 'No'

answers. So the Detective might ask 'Toby, does the killer have blond hair?' After asking all three questions, the Detective then has to accuse one of the players of being the Killer. The accused player has to open his hands. If he has the paper, the Detective wins and the Killer becomes the new Detective. If the Detective is wrong, he has to go again.

Players cannot lie, but they should try their hardest not to give away the Killer's identity.

INVESTIGATE THE CRIME SCENE

This hotel room has been burgled. Study the photograph of the crime scene below for 30 seconds and then answer the questions over the page. Try to give the police as much information as you can.

INVESTIGATE THE CRIME SCENE CONTINUED ...

Answer the questions below without turning back to look at the picture on page 15. Check your answers on page 62.

1. When was the photograph taken?

   A. During the day
   B. At night

2. There are two pictures hanging on the wall. What are they of?

3. Where is the football?

4. Where is the rucksack?

5. Is the rucksack open or closed?

6. One of the patio doors is broken. Is it the door on the right or the left?

7. Where is the broken glass?

   A. Inside the room
   B. On the patio

8. How many tennis rackets are there in the room?

9. Is the suitcase open or closed?

10. Which drawer has been removed from the chest of drawers?

   A. Top
   B. Middle
   C. Bottom

FIND THE MISSING NUMBER

Each animal in this grid represents a number – either 1, 2, 3 or 4.

If you add up the numbers in any row or column, you get the total at the end of that row or column.

For example three elephants, and a tiger equals 5, and two elephants a tiger and a lion equals 8.

Work out which animal represents which number, and then work out the missing number.

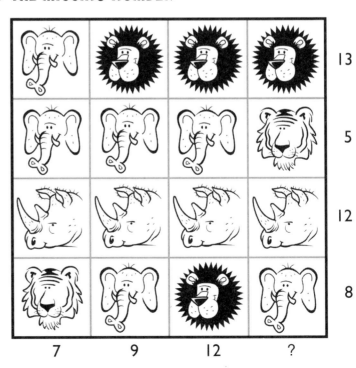

SUMMER SAFARI

What has the explorer discovered in the rainforest?

SUMMER DAYS AT PUZZLE PARK

The sun's out and you've got a whole day of fun ahead at Puzzle Park.
Check your answers on page 63.

SWINGS AND ROUNDABOUTS

Each of these circles represents a fun thing to do at the park. The letters represent people.

Where the circles cross over each other, the people like to do more than one thing. For example, D, likes the roundabout and lying on the grass, but does not like the slide or the swings.

Can you spot who loves the slide and the swings but does not like the roundabout or lying on the grass?

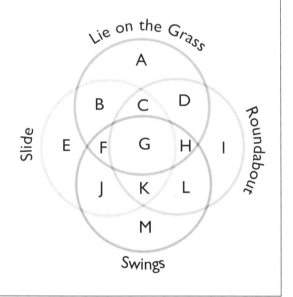

FRUIT SHAKE AT THE PARK CAFÉ

Can you unscramble the flavours of the fruit shakes on the café's board?
Which flavour is the odd one out?

MENU

1. CKURNRABTLAC
2. NBAAAN
3. PRABSYRER
4. RWSARRETBY
5. HLOOATCEC
6. EAHPC

NUT CRACKERS

Only two of these pictures of a squirrel with his lunch are exactly the same.

Can you spot the matching pair?

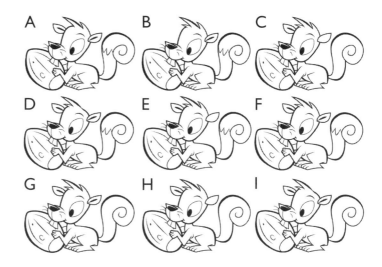

TIME TO GO, TOMMY!

Can you find Tommy and tell him it is time to go home for his tea? Tommy is wearing shorts and gloves but he isn't wearing a hat. He has long sleeves on his T-shirt. Can you spot him?

SEASIDE CHEF SCHOOL

You're 'shore' to like these delicious recipes.

OCTOPASTA PERFECTION

These wriggling octopuses are really delicious and very easy to make. Here's how to make enough to feed two hungry sailors.

You will need:

- 250 g dried spaghetti
- 8 frankfurters • a pinch of salt
- a pan of boiling water
- 1 small jar tomato pasta sauce
- 2 tablespoons grated cheese

1. Open the packet (or jar) of frankfurters. Chop each of the frankfurters into five equally sized pieces using a table knife and then put them to one side.

2. Break the strands of spaghetti in half.

3. Push eight strands of spaghetti about halfway into each of the sausage pieces so that the spaghetti is firmly attached.

4. Ask an adult to put them and the rest of the spaghetti into a large pan of boiling water with the salt.

5. Boil the spaghetti and sausages together following the instructions on the pack.

6. When the spaghetti is cooked, ask an adult to drain it very carefully using a colander. Put the colander to one side.

7. Heat the pasta sauce according to the directions on the jar.

8. Dish out your octopasta into two large bowls and then pour on your sauce.

9. Sprinkle over the grated cheese and serve. Yum!

HOT BANANA BOATS

The mixture of hot banana, melted marshmallows and gooey chocolate makes a delicious pud.

You will need:

• 4 big bananas • 2 tablespoons mini marshmallows (or bigger ones torn into bits) • 2 tablespoons chocolate chips

1. Ask an adult to preheat the oven to 190 °C/Gas Mark 5.

2. Hold one of the bananas so that its curved outer edge is pressed against the table.

3. Push the tip of your table knife half way into the curved edge of the banana.

4. Make a slit from just below the stalk until just before the end of the banana.

5. Repeat this for the other bananas.

6. Cram as many chocolate chips and mini marshmallows as you can into each banana. Any that don't fit, eat yourself!

7. Wrap each of your stuffed bananas tightly in tin foil.

8. Ask an adult to put your bananas into the oven for 10 minutes and to take them out when they are done.

9. Leave the bananas to cool for 10 minutes and then unwrap and munch.

Warning. These bananas are seriously hot. Make sure you get an adult to check them before you start unwrapping them or you could burn your hands and mouth.

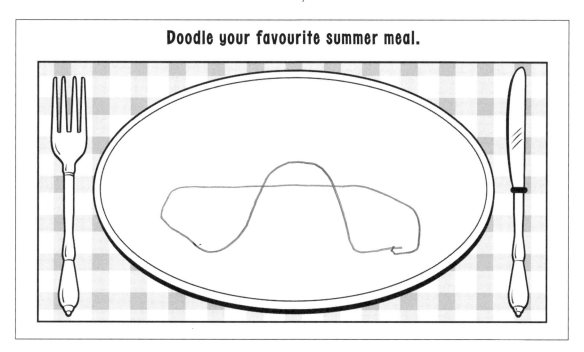

Doodle your favourite summer meal.

SUMMER SPYMASTER

Keep your secret missions secret this summer with these cool codes.

TOP-SECRET MESSAGES

When you're on your summer holidays and relying on postcards or emails to send your fellow agents instructions, it's important to be able to keep your messages top secret.

All super spies know that the best way to keep a message secret is to write it in code.

CODING MADE EASY

An easy code to use is to move each letter in your message to the next letter in the alphabet.

For example:
MEET MONDAY AT SIX

becomes:
NFFU NPOEBZ BU TJY

To make this code trickier, try getting rid of the spaces between the letters:

NFFUNPOEBZBUTJY

CODE BREAKER

A secret agent has written three messages in the code above. Can you crack the code and answer the following questions?

1. Are the files hot or cold?

2. What does he want for his dinner?

Check your answers on page 63.

Message One

UIFGJMFTBSFJOUIFGSJEHF

Message Two

HJWFUIFNUPNZNVN

Message Three

UFMMNVNJXBOUTBVTBHFT GPSEJOOFS

BUILD YOUR OWN UNBREAKABLE-CODE MACHINE

Make code wheels for you and a friend so that you can decode each other's messages. Here's how.

You will need:

- a sheet of white paper • a pencil
- scissors • a blob of modelling clay
- a pen • a paper fastener
- some paper for your message

1. Place the paper over the templates at the bottom of the page.

2. Trace around both circles, using your pencil. Mark the alphabet on circle A.

3. Cut out both of your circles, cutting out the black squares on circle B.

4. Place circle B on top of circle A so that the crosses lie on top of one another. Place them on top of a lump of modelling clay and push a paper fastener through the crosses into the clay.

5. Split the fastener at the back to keep the circles together.

6. To use your wheel, turn the top circle so that box **Z** shows the letter you want to write, then write the letter revealed by box **1** on to your paper. For example, when 'A' is showing in box **Z**, box **1** shows the letter 'U', so you write the letter 'U'. Do the same for each letter of the message you want to code.

7. To use a different code, use boxes **2** or **3** instead of **1**. Make sure your friend has a code wheel and agree which box you are going to use before you send your message.

DECODING MESSAGES

To decode a message, turn the top circle so that the box you agreed reveals the written letter and then write the letter showing in box **Z** on your paper.

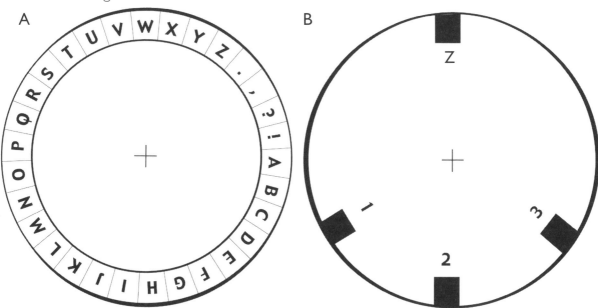

THE REAL ROBINSON CRUSOE

Four long years alone on a desert island – could you survive?

You may know the story of Robinson Crusoe – shipwrecked on an island. What you may not know is that this story is based on the adventures of a man called Alexander Selkirk.

RUNNING AWAY TO SEA

Selkirk was the son of a shoemaker and ran away from home to get rich working at sea. Selkirk went to work on a ship as a kind of pirate. The crew stole the cargo of enemy ships'. It was an exciting but very dangerous job. The ship sailed in rough seas all over the world.

In 1704, Alexander Selkirk worked on a ship called the *Cinque Ports,* which sailed around the coast of South America. After a few battles and bad weather, Selkirk was convinced that the ship was in need of repair. His captain disagreed and refused to stop sailing. Selkirk demanded to be put ashore on the next island, rather than sail on a ship that he thought wasn't safe.

CAST ASHORE

The captain agreed, and Selkirk was put ashore on the island of a Tierra – over 600 kilometres off the coast of Chile in South America. He was only allowed to take a few basic tools and supplies from the ship. Selkirk decided he would wait on the island for the next passing ship to take him home.

ALL ALONE

Alone on the island, Selkirk kept a fire burning on a hill in the hope that a passing ship might see it, but none came. Months turned into years as he waited. His supplies soon ran out, but luckily there were fruits and vegetables growing on the island and goats for meat and milk. He even made clothes from the goats' skins when his own fell apart.

One day he saw two ships and he rushed to the shore to meet them, but the ships belonged to the king's enemies and he had to hide. He didn't speak to or see another human for four years.

ON THE HORIZON

In 1709, he spotted a sail, and an English flag. A ship! Selkirk looked like a wild man, with a long beard and wearing animal skins. Amazingly one of the ship's crewmen recognized him from the *Cinque Ports* and he was taken aboard.

When he returned home, Selkirk met a writer, who wrote of his adventures for a magazine. Later, another writer used Selkirk's story for a book, calling the hero not Alexander Selkirk … but Robinson Crusoe!

ISLAND ADVENTURES

Can you survive on this tropical island? Check your answers on page 63.

CROP CONUNDRUM

On your desert island you need food to eat, so you decide to grow some coconuts, bananas and mangoes. You divide up the island into plots. Each plot of fruit can only share borders with plots of different fruit.

Can you write in the name of the right crop in each empty plot, and work out what crop you are going to have in the plots marked **A** and **B**?

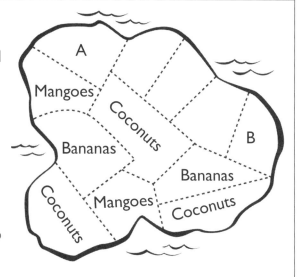

ISLAND ATTACK!

Join the dots to see what is chasing the castaway.

Doodle your own ingenious invention.

CROSSED WIRES

The inventor has tangled the cables to his inventions. Can you work out which plug belongs to which invention? Check your answers on page 63.

Robobutler

Chocotoaster

Instajellymatic

TOP OF THE LEAGUE

Take your team from non-league to the world champions!

Each player must place a coin on the Non-League Start. Take it in turns to spin the spinner and move your coin. Follow any instructions on the square that you land on. To become the Champions of a league, you must land exactly on the 'Champions!' square. If the number you spin is too high, you must wait for your next turn.

CHAMPIONS!
Go to League One Start.

Lose by 5 goals at home. Go back 3 spaces.

Star player injured. Go back 1 space.

Come back from 2 goals down to win. Go up 3 spaces.

CHAMPIONS!
Go to League Two Start.

Win at home. Go up 1 space.

Win 3 games in a row. Go up 2 spaces.

Your star player's mum won't let him play. Miss a turn.

League Two
START

Non-League
START

CHAMPIONS!

Go to World League Start.

Score a winning goal in the final minute. Go up 2 spaces.

Play in a charity league. Swap places with a player ahead of you.

WORLD CHAMPIONS!

Player banned for fighting. Go back to League Two start.

Star player transfers to rival squad. Miss a turn.

League One

START

World League

START

Cut out the spinner and push a toothpick through the middle. To spin your spinner, hold the toothpick upright on your playing surface and spin it between your thumb and index finger. The number at the top of the spinner when it stops spinning tells you the number of spaces you should move.

SPINNER

Design the ultimate go-kart track for the drivers to race on.

BACK OF SPINNER

GO-KART GRAND PRIX

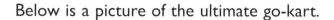

Below is a picture of the ultimate go-kart.

Using the squares in the grid below to help you, can you copy it?

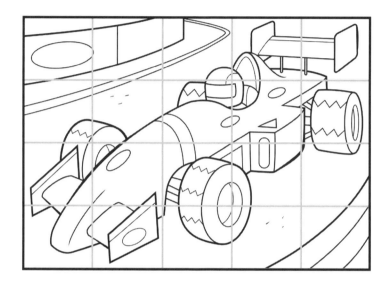

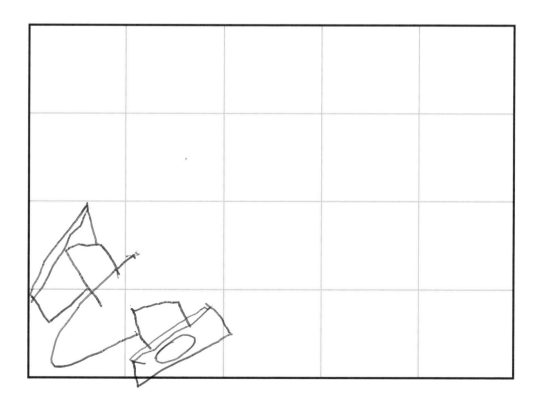

CREATE YOUR OWN SUMMER COMIC STRIP

Learn how to draw Doodles the Dog and then make him the star of your own comic capers.

To draw Doodles, simply follow the instructions below. Practise drawing him on rough paper before starring him in the comic strips opposite.

You will need:

- rough paper • a pencil
- a permanent black pen
- a rubber • felt-tip pens

1. Use a pencil to draw the basic shape by drawing circles to show his head and body.

2. Draw more shapes for his nose and tail and add his legs.

3. Use your black pen to draw the outline around the shapes. Leave areas blank where the different parts attach to his body.

4. Add Doodles' eyes and the insides of his ears.

5. Leave your picture to dry, then rub out all of your pencil lines using your rubber. Use your felt pens to colour him in.

Now you have your finished Doodles, use him to create some crazy comic strips on the opposite page. What adventures will he have this summer?

THE ADVENTURES OF DOODLES

YOUR COMIC STRIPS!

STAY COOL!

Learn to say, 'Hello, how are you?', 'It's really hot' and 'Where is the beach?' in six different languages. A guide to how to pronounce the words is given in *italics* below.

FRENCH

Bonjour, comment ça va?
Bonjhoor, common sa va?

Il fait très chaud!
Eel fay tray show!

Où est la plage?
Ooh ai la plahj?

GERMAN

Hallo! Wie geht's?
Ha-llo, vee gates?

Es ist sehr heiß!
Ess ist zair heiss!

Wo ist der Strand?
Vo ist dair shtrant?

SPANISH

¡Hola! Qué tal?
Oh-lah, kay tal?

Hace mucho calor!
Athay moochoh calaw!

Donde esta la playa?
Donday estah la plyah?

PORTUGUESE

Olá! Tudo bem?
Oh-lah! Toodoh baym?

Faz muito calor!
Fazjh mweetu cahlaw!

Onde é a praia?
On-duh ay ah prajah?

RUSSIAN

Privet, kak ti?
Preevyet, kak tiy?

Oi, kak zharko.
Oi, kak zharrko.

A gde plyazh?
A gd-yay plyazh?

ITALIAN

Ciao! Come stai?
Chow! Comeh stye?

Fa molto caldo!
Fa molto caaldo!

Dov'e' la spiaggia?
Doh-veh la spee-a-gee-ah?

HIT THE BEACH

There is always lots of fun to be had at the beach. There are 20 shells in this picture. Can you find them all? Check your answer on page 63.

SOGGY SUMMER GAMES

Even the sunniest summers have the odd rainy day. Here are some great games to keep you busy until the sun comes out.

DON'T LOSE YOUR MARBLES

You will need:
- two to six players
- a long piece of string
- 13 small marbles • 1 big marble for each player to use as a Shooter

1. Use your string to form the outline of a circle on the floor roughly 1 metre across. This is your marble arena.

2. Place the 13 small marbles in the centre of the circle. It's up to you how you position them – you could arrange them in a cluster, or even have them scattered randomly around the circle.

3. The youngest player goes first. Kneel at any point outside the circle, and lean inwards so that the hand that is holding the Shooter is inside the circle.

4. To shoot your marble, place your knuckles on the floor, with the Shooter held in your curled index finger.

5. Use your thumb to flick the Shooter at a smaller marble in the circle.

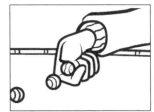

The aim is to knock these marbles out of the circle, while keeping the Shooter inside the circle. Each marble that is knocked out is worth one point. If your Shooter stays inside the circle, you get to shoot again, starting from where it landed.

6. Your turn ends when you either fail to knock out any marbles, or if the Shooter ends up outside the circle. It is then the turn of the player on your left.

7. Keep playing until all the marbles have been knocked out of the circle. The player with the most points, wins.

CRAZY CARD-TOSS CAPERS

You will need:

- at least two players
- a pack of cards • a hat or large bowl

TOP TECHNIQUE

1. To hold the card, place one of the corners between your index finger and your middle finger with your knuckles bent. Rotate your hand at the wrist bringing the card towards you and then flick it forward, at the same time releasing your grip on the card. Try to flick your wrist sharply outwards so that your card flies forwards and away from you.

2. Practise shooting your cards at different targets around the room and when you think you have mastered the skill, it is time to play.

3. Place the hat or bowl on the floor. Players should sit or stand roughly 3 metres away from it.

4. Divide a pack of cards up evenly among the number of players.

5. Each player takes it in turns to try and flick one of his cards into the hat. If the card goes in, he gets another go, otherwise play passes to the next player. Keep score as you go.

6. The winner of each round is the player who gets the most cards into the hat. The first player to win five rounds is the card-toss champion.

SUMMER AT THE CIRCUS

Roll up, roll up! The circus has come to town.
Tackle the puzzles and check your answers on page 63.

PUT UP THE BIG TOP

Can you work out which of the boxes has all of the right pieces to build this circus tent?

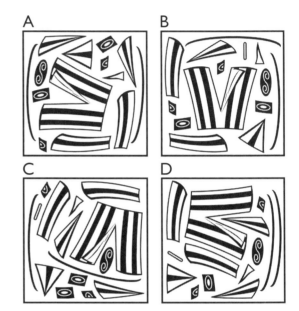

THE HUMAN CANNON BALL

Last time Harry was fired from the cannon, he landed 3 metres beyond and 2 metres to the left of the net. For his next attempt, should he move the cannon 3 metres further away and 2 metres to the right, or 3 metres towards the net and 2 metres to the left?

FIND THE SQUARES

All of the squares below can be found in the picture of this super-strong man.

Can you find out where each square belongs? Write down the letter of the column and the number of the row in which it appears.

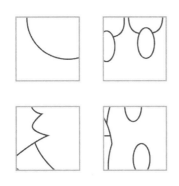

Top Tip. The squares aren't necessarily the right way up.

CLOWNING AROUND

This juggling clown has all of his balls in the air.

There are seven pairs of balls that are exactly the same and only one ball that is unique.

Can you find the ball that doesn't have an identical pair?

CIRCUS SKILLS

Long summer holidays are the perfect time to master the art of juggling to wow your friends.

JUGGLING BASICS

1. Begin with one ball. Stand with your arms bent and your hands shoulder-width apart. Throw the ball from one hand to the other, and back. Make sure that the ball reaches the height of your eyes with every throw. Keep throwing one ball until you manage to throw it and catch it the same way every time without thinking.

2. Now add another ball. Hold one ball in each hand. Throw the first ball up as you did in step 1. When the first ball has reached eye height, and is just about to come down, throw the second ball. This will leave your hand empty just in time to catch the first ball. This is called the 'exchange'. Practise this over and over again until you get into a rhythm.

3. Now you are ready to try three balls. Hold two balls in one hand and one in the other. The action is exactly the same as the exchange you practised in step **2** with two balls. Throw the first ball, then throw the second ball just before you catch the first. This time you need to throw the third ball just before you catch the second. This is called a 'pass'.

4. To begin with, doing one pass will be quite difficult, but try to increase the number of passes each time you practise to become an expert juggler. Once you've managed three passes in a row, you are juggling!

Top Tip. Keep your eyes straight ahead, looking at the top of your throws.

A BAG OF TRICKS

When you're comfortable with three balls you can look at bringing in some tricks.

TRICK TWO: One-hand wonder

Hold two balls in one hand. Throw the first ball straight up. Move your hand to the right and throw the second ball up before quickly moving your hand back to catch the first. Catch the first and throw it again as you move to catch the second. The balls should be going straight up and down while your hand moves from side to side.

TRICK ONE: Cool crossover

Start with two balls in one hand and one in the other. Throw the first ball (from the hand with two balls) straight up, a little higher than normal. Then throw the other two at the same time so they cross over above your head. Catch the first ball with the hand you threw it from and then continue to juggle as normal.

THE GOLDEN RULE

Once you've learned how to juggle, you will never forget how to do it. The key to improvement is practice.

HANDS UP FOR HANJIE

Had enough of playing 'I spy'?
Try out these travel games and time will fly . . .

Hanjie is a brilliant Japanese drawing puzzle in which you use numbers to work out which squares to shade in a grid. As you shade in more and more squares the picture reveals itself.

The numbers tell you how many squares to shade in a particular row or column. For example, the numbers 3, 3 at the side of a row tells you that you need to shade in a group of three squares together and then leave a gap of at least one square before shading in another group of three squares somewhere in that row.

HOW TO HANJIE

Take a look at the puzzle below to see how it's done, and then have a go at the Hanjie puzzle on the opposite page.

1. As the grid is five squares across you know that any row with a 5 next to it is all shaded in.

2. Fill in the columns that have 3,1,4 above them. Each of these columns is 10 squares long so that you can be sure that if you shade 3, 1 and then 4 squares together leaving a gap between each block, you have used up the column.

3. Then there are three rows with just a 3 by them, so we can complete three groups of three.

4. Finally, complete the 5 in the middle column and the two 2s in the bottom row to finish your Hanjie.

HIGH-FLYING HANJIE

Have a go at this Hanjie puzzle and watch the time fly by. Some squares have been done for you. Check your answers on page 64.

Top Tips. If a Hanjie puzzle is 10 squares wide (like this one) and a column or row has the number 10 by it you can shade in all 10 squares in that row or column.

Sometimes you will know that a square is definitely NOT shaded. In that case, put a little dot in it to remind you, it will help you out later!

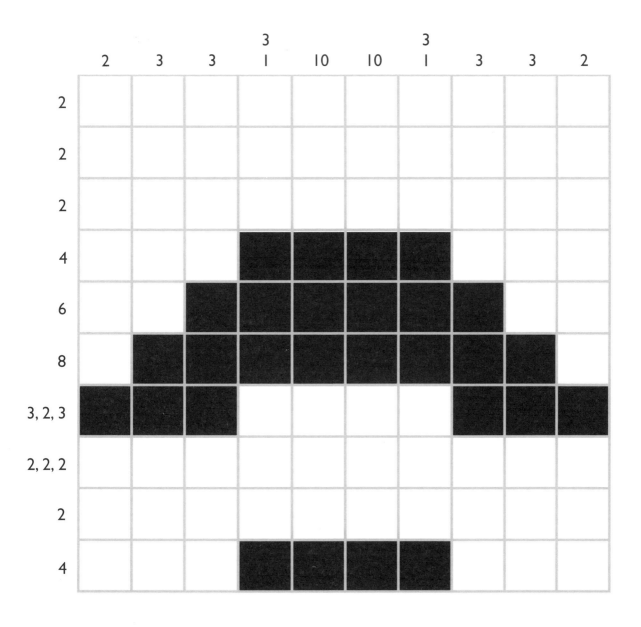

ULTIMATE I-SPY

Keep your eyes peeled to make long, boring road journeys fly by.

You can play this game with as many people as you like. When each item on the list below is spotted, write the initials of the person who spotted it first in the box.

When all the items have been spotted the spotter who has spotted the most, wins.

1. A yellow car		16. A horse box	
2. A post box		17. A traffic jam	
3. A tree with no leaves		18. A sports car	
4. A river		19. Someone running	
5. A set of traffic lights		20. A sign for a theme park	
6. An electricity pylon		21. A service station	
7. A red lorry		22. A hot-air balloon	
8. A dead animal		23. Graffiti	
9. A cow		24. A child on roller skates	
10. A church		25. A woman in a purple hat	
11. A castle		26. A police car	
12. A flag		27. A broken-down vehicle	
13. A bird of prey		28. A bridge	
14. A tractor		29. A boat (of any kind)	
15. A caravan		30. An aeroplane taking off	

WHAT WILL YOU BE?

A movie star? A footballer? A president? An astronaut? Take this quiz then turn the page to find out what your answers say about your future!

1. What is your idea of a fun way to spend a summer afternoon?

   A. Playing computer games
   B. Climbing a mountain
   C. Making a model from a kit

2. You're hungry, what do you do?

   A. Order a pizza online
   B. Make yourself a sandwich
   C. Persuade Mum to make a snack

3. How would you like to celebrate your birthday?

   A. Paintballing
   B. Go-karting or jet-skiing
   C. A trip to a theme park

4. What would you get your friend for a special birthday?

   A. Make them a CD of music
   B. Get them a new pair of trainers
   C. Make a mini movie about them

5. You get lost in the woods. What do you do?

   A. Use the map tool on your mobile
   B. Retrace your steps
   C. Call for help

6. What kind of movie would be your choice out of these?

   A. A science fiction movie
   B. An action movie
   C. A feature-length cartoon

7. You discover your computer doesn't work! What do you do?

   A. Fix it straight away
   B. Do something else until it's fixed
   C. Borrow someone else's

8. You're playing a game with your younger cousin. What do you do?

   A. Teach him how to play properly
   B. Beat him every time
   C. Let him win to keep him happy

9. You're camping out in the countryside. What do you do?

   A. Take a games console
   B. Build a survival shelter
   C. Organize a scavenger hunt

10. Which of these people would you most like to meet?

   A. Bill Gates
   B. Usain Bolt
   C. Will Smith

WHAT YOUR ANSWERS SAY ABOUT YOU

Count up how many times you have answered **A**, **B** or **C** in the quiz on page 45. Read on to reveal what your answers say about your future.

Mostly As

You are a techno whizz.

You love technology and are good at using it. If humans ever get to Mars you'll be on the first spacecraft to land. You would make a great scientist, a doctor, a computer games designer, or even an astronaut. Your brilliant mind could lead to you inventing cool things that could make you a very rich man!

Mostly Bs

You are an action hero.

Brave and adventurous, you could be an explorer, a soldier or a film stuntman. You like to win, which could help you take your chosen sport to the highest level – a World Cup maybe, or the Olympic Games. Your practical mind could help you to lead expeditions to far away places.

Mostly Cs

You are a creative genius.

Artistic and fun to be around, you could be an actor, a director or a musician. You like talking to people and making them feel good, so people like to be around you. You're comfortable in the spotlight and are looking forward to people queueing up for your latest film, your new album or just for your autograph!

WACKY SUMMER SPORTS

Read on to find out about some weird and wacky sports
you could get up to this summer.

BELGIUM: Bathtub sailing

Is it a dinghy? Is it a canoe? No … it is the International Regatta of the Bathtubs. Held in the town of Dinant in August, hopefuls in fancy dress race their bathtubs down the River Meuse hoping to reach the finish line first.

Pelting spectators and other competitors with buckets of water is encouraged, but fitting any kind of engine is strictly forbidden.

USA: Hot-dog eating

Every 4th of July at a restaurant on Coney Island in New York, people from all over the world come to watch 20 competitors compete in the annual hot-dog eating contest. Contestants must eat as many hot dogs and buns as they can in just 12 minutes. Winning contestants often manage to stuff their faces with more than 50 hot dogs in the time.

Warning: This sort of extreme eating takes lots of training, and should not be attempted at home.

ENGLAND: Cheese rolling

At the end of May in a small town in Gloucestershire a group of brave people gather to chase a large, round cheese down a very steep hill. During the event the enormous cheese can reach speeds of 112 kilometres per hour. Competitors have been known to break bones in this cheesy quest.

WALES: Bog snorkelling

Every August, a small village in Wales hosts the international bog-snorkelling championships. People come from all over the world to swim two lengths through the thick, brown water as fast as they can wearing flippers and snorkels. One competitor from Australia described her experience as like 'swimming through pea soup.' Yuck!

SUMMER FUN ON THE HIGH STREET

Have a top time in town with these brilliant puzzles
Check your answers on page 64.

WHERE TO MEET?

You are meeting a friend on the High Street, but you've forgotten where! You remember it wasn't at either end of the street and it wasn't at any shop that began with 'B'. It wasn't next door to the hairdresser or opposite the bookshop, so where were you supposed to meet?

You meet your friend, then cross the street and spend ten minutes in the shop opposite. Then you turn left out of that shop and go three shops along and pop in to that shop. Then you cross the street again to the shop opposite. Did you buy a book, a belt or a banana there?

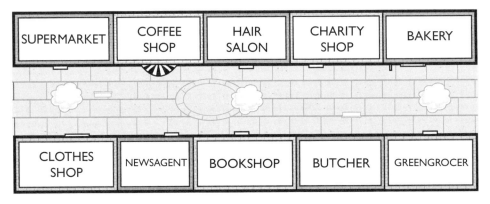

JUNK FOOD JUMBLE

A burger, some fries, an ice cream and a yummy thick vanilla shake – they're so unhealthy, yet so tasty.

Fill in the blank boxes so that each row and each column in the grid has only one of each junk food item.

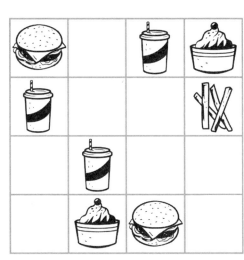

SPOT THE DIFFERENCE

The monkeys from the local zoo have escaped and invaded the greengrocers.
Can you spot the 10 differences between these two pictures of mayhem?

BUILD YOUR OWN SUMMER SPACE ROCKET

Rockets are really simple machines – just a tube filled with fuel, a nose cone and some fins. The fuel makes air rush out of the bottom end, and the nose cone and fins help the tube to fly straight as it shoots into the air!

You will need:

- a fizzy aspirin or vitamin C tablet
- a film canister with lid • scissors
- a piece of thin card • sticky tape

PREPARING FOR LAUNCH

1. Cut out the shapes opposite using a pair of scissors.

2. Give your rocket a name that is out of this world and write it on the circle, avoiding the shaded quarter.

3. Cut the shaded quarter out of the circle, and tape the straight edges together to form a cone.

4. Place the film canister on the long edge of the piece of card and roll the paper up to make a tight tube. Secure it in place using sticky tape as shown with the lid at the bottom.

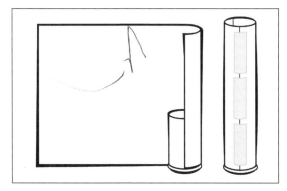

5. Attach the cone to the top of your rocket using sticky tape.

6. Fold the four fins along the dotted lines and then tape the folded edges to the base of your rocket as shown.

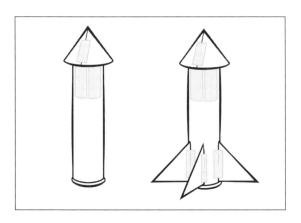

6 ... 5 ... 4 ... 3 ... 2 ...

7. Now you are ready to launch your rocket. Turn it upside-down and take the lid off the canister. Fill the canister two-thirds full of water. Then drop in half a fizzy aspirin and quickly replace the lid.

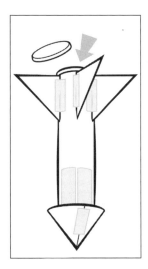

Cut out the pieces below and fold along the dotted lines.

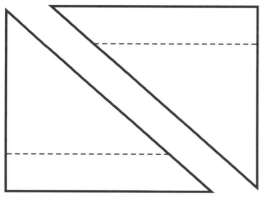

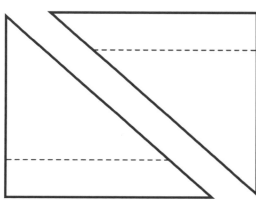

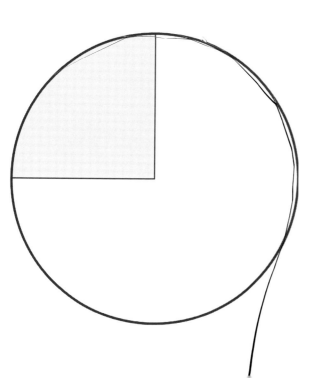

... WE HAVE LIFT OFF!

8. Put your rocket back the right way up, stand well back and wait for blast off!

Top Tip. Make more than one rocket and have a competition to see whose rocket shoots the highest. Experiment with different shapes of cone and fin to see if these will give your rocket the edge against the competition.

Doodle the launching rocket.

Back of the rocket.

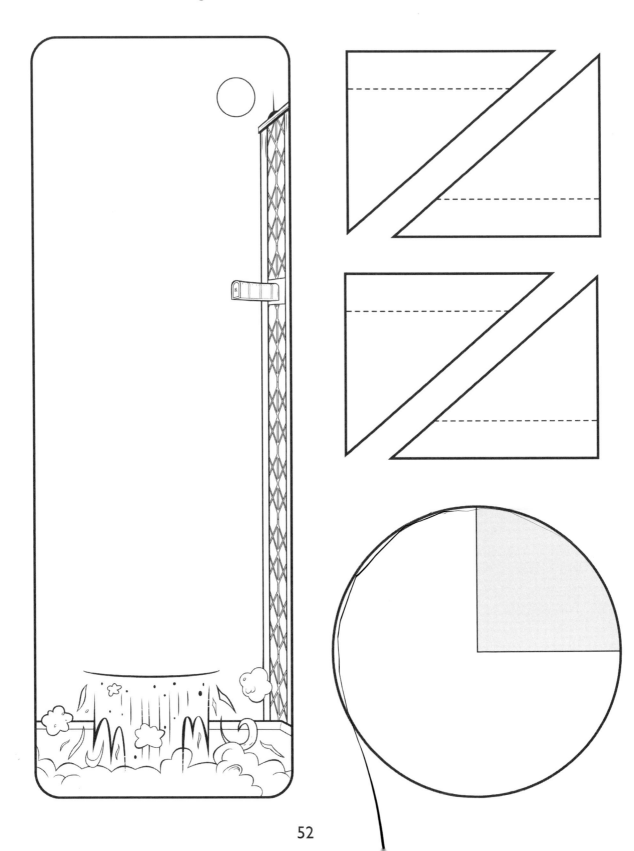

52

SUMMER AT THE THEME PARK

Can you find your way around the rides at the theme park?
Check your answers on page 64.

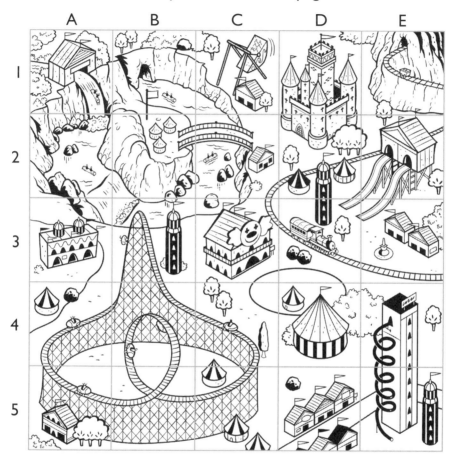

Start at the square indicated by the number and the letter in brackets, then find your way around the park following the directions on the compass below.

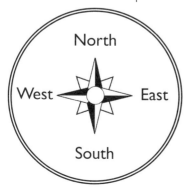

Example: The Giant Swing (**1C**). If you walk 2 South, 2 East, 2 South, 1 West, 1 North you end up at the Big Top (**4D**).

1. Starting from the Spiral Slide (**5E**)

   2 North, 2 West, 1 South, 1 East

2. Starting from the Rickety Bridge (**2C**)

   2 South, 2 West, 3 North

3. Starting from the Coaster (**5A**)

   2 North, 4 East, 1 North

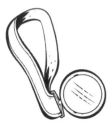

THE ULTIMATE SUMMER PENTATHLON

A pentathlon is an athletic competition made up of five events. When the sun is shining, get out into the park and hold your own pentathlon. You will need at least three players. The player who wins the most events is the ultimate champion.

EVENT ONE: The standing long jump

Mark a line on the grass using some string. Take it in turns to stand behind the line, and jump as far as you can over the line with no run up. Mark the spot you land with a twig. The person who jumps the furthest is the winner.

EVENT TWO: The ping-pong put

This event is like the shot put – players throw a heavy metal ball as far as they can. In this event you must use a ping-pong ball. Hold the ball in the palm of your hand level with your jaw. Push your arm forward as strongly as you can and release the ball – the person who throws the furthest is the winner.

EVENT THREE: Puff ball

Mark two lines on the ground, roughly 3 metres apart. Ask each player to place his ping-pong ball on the first line, and kneel down behind it. You must race to get your ping-pong ball from the first line to the second and back again using only the power of your puff. The first to the finish is the winner.

EVENT FOUR: The high jump

Two players hold a length of rope or string between them, keeping it very low to the ground. The jumper must jump over the rope. If he manages it, the rope is raised higher off the ground to make the jump more challenging. The person who can jump the highest, wins.

EVENT FIVE: Target bowls

Drop a tennis ball on to the ground and take two large paces away. Mark this spot with a stone. Each player should kneel by this stone and roll a ping-pong ball towards the tennis ball. The aim is to get as close to the tennis ball as possible without touching it. The player that rolls his ball closest to the tennis ball is the winner.

Oh, no! What is the shot put going to land on?

COOL COOKIE MEDALS

Are you going for gold, silver, bronze or chocolate chip? Make these big cookie medals and you'll have something to play for.

You will need:

- 100 g chocolate chips
- 125 g melted butter • 175 g sugar
- 1 beaten egg • 150 g plain flour
- ½ teaspoon baking powder
- a pinch of salt
- 4 x 50 cm lengths of ribbon

To make four medals:

1. Ask an adult to preheat the oven to 190 °C/Gas mark 5.

2. Grease a large, square baking sheet by dipping a piece of kitchen paper in the butter and rubbing it all over the sheet until you have covered it all.

3. Add the sugar to a mixing bowl and pour the rest of the melted butter on top. Mix this together with a wooden spoon.

4. Pour in the beaten egg and mix it together until the mixture is all combined.

5. Add the flour, baking powder and pinch of salt, then mix together.

6. For each medal, dollop three large

spoonfuls of mixture in each quarter of your baking sheet. Allow the mixture to spread out into big circles.

7. Arrange the chocolate chips to make the numbers 1, 2, 3 and 4 on top of each cookie.

8. Ask an adult to put the cookies into the oven for 10 to 12 minutes.

9. Ask an adult to take the cookies out of the oven.

10. While the cookies are still warm and soft, make holes 1 centimetre from the top edge of each cookie using a skewer. Make the holes big enough to thread your ribbons through.

11. Leave the cookies to cool.

12. When the cookie medals are cool and have hardened, thread your ribbon through the holes and tie a knot in them to make a loop.

13. Hang your cookie around your neck and enjoy.

AHOY THERE!

Test your seafaring strategy skills with these boat-tastic brainteasers.
Check your answers on page 64.

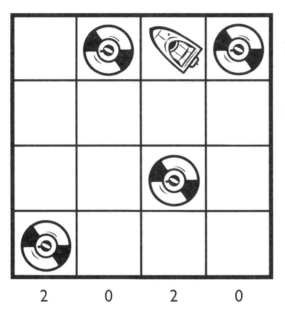

OH BUOY!

2 All the boats are coming back to the harbour and you are the harbour master. Each buoy must

0 have at least one boat horizontally or vertically next to it.

1 The numbers tell you how many boats there can be in each row or column.

1 Can you make sure each buoy has a boat?

BATTLESHIP BRAINTEASER

There are a total of three cruisers, three launches and three buoys in this grid. Two buoys, two cruisers and a launch have been revealed for you. Can you find the rest?

The numbers tell you how many squares or groups of occupied squares there are in each row or column.

For example the numbers 3, 2 tell you there is a group of three squares together and a group of two squares together, with at least one empty square between them.

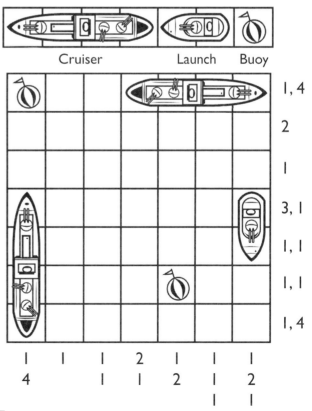

WORLD MENU MADNESS

Solve these menu muddles and then check
your answers on page 64.

MEATBALL MAYHEM

How many meatballs can you spot in the Italian restaurant?

WHERE IN THE WORLD?

Link the countries to their delicious delicacies. The first one is done for you.

Lasagne	France
Jellyfish with noodles	Spain
Grilled guinea pig	Italy
Frogs' legs	Indonesia
Frankfurter	Peru
Bat stew	United Kingdom
Tortilla	China
Toad in the hole	Germany

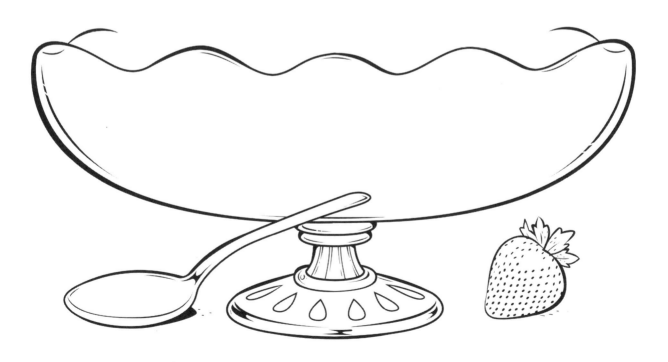

Draw the ultimate ice-cream sundae.

THE SUMMER OF FUN

Keep a record of your summer of fun by drawing, sticking or painting pictures of all the exciting things you have been doing this summer.

ALL THE ANSWERS

SUMMER SPACE GETAWAY
pages 4 and 5

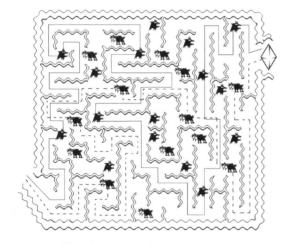

To the crystal. ———————

To the spacecraft. ------------

ANCHORS AWAY
page 7

Boat **1** belongs to anchor **C**.
Boat **2** belongs to anchor **A**.
Boat **3** belongs to anchor **B**.

AWESOME ANIMAL QUIZ
pages 8 and 9

1. A, 2. B, 3. B, 4. B, 5. D, 6. C, 7. D,
8. A, 9. C, 10. B, 11. A, 12. B

BOX CLEVER
page 12

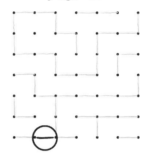

CRIME SCENE INVESTIGATION
pages 15 and 16

1. A
2. Planet Earth and the Sphinx in Egypt.
3. On the pillow.
4. At the foot of the bed.
5. Closed.
6. On the right.
7. A
8. One.
9. Open.
10. Top.

FIND THE MISSING NUMBER
page 16

 = 1    = 3

? = 10

 = 2   = 4

SUMMER DAYS AT PUZZLE PARK
pages 18 and 19

J loves the slide and the swings, but does not like the roundabout or lying on the grass.

BLACKCURRANT, BANANA, RASPBERRY, STRAWBERRY, CHOCOLATE, PEACH.

Chocolate is the odd one out as the rest are fruits.

Squirrel **C** and squirrel **H**.

CROSSED WIRES
page 27

Switch **A** belongs to the Robobutler.
Switch **B** belongs to the Chocotoaster.
Switch **C** belongs to the Instajellymatic.

HIT THE BEACH
page 35

CODE BREAKER
page 22

One: THE FILES ARE IN THE FRIDGE.

Two: GIVE THEM TO MY MUM.

Three: TELL HER I WANT SAUSAGES FOR DINNER.

I. The files are cold.
2. Sausages.

SUMMER AT THE CIRCUS
pages 38 and 39

Box **C**

3 metres further away and 2 metres to the right.

The pieces match the following squares:
F2, F3, C5 and **D4**

Ball **14** is the odd one out.

ISLAND ADVENTURES
page 25

A = Bananas   **B** = Coconuts

HANDS UP FOR HANJIE
pages 42 and 43

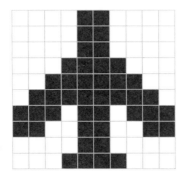

SUMMER FUN ON THE HIGH STREET
pages 48 and 49

You met your friend at the newsagent and then went to the greengrocers and bought a banana.

SUMMER AT THE THEME PARK
page 53

1. The Big Top (**4D**)
2. Thunder River (**1A**)
3. The Slip and Slide (**2E**)

AHOY THERE!
page 57

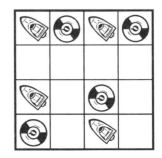

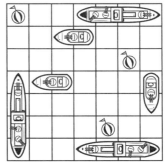

WORLD MENU MADNESS
page 58

There are 30 meatballs in the picture.

Jellyfish with noodles – China
Grilled guinea pig – Peru
Frogs' legs – France
Frankfurter – Germany
Bat stew – Indonesia
Tortilla – Spain
Toad in the hole – United Kingdom